STUDY GUIDE

THE
DEBORAH
ANOINTING

MICHELLE McCLAIN-WALTERS

CHARISMA
HOUSE

Most CHARISMA HOUSE BOOK GROUP products are available at special quantity discounts for bulk purchase for sales promotions, premiums, fund-raising, and educational needs. For details, write Charisma House Book Group, 600 Rinehart Road, Lake Mary, Florida 32746, or telephone (407) 333-0600.

THE DEBORAH ANOINTING STUDY GUIDE
  by Michelle McClain-Walters
Published by Charisma House
Charisma Media/Charisma House Book Group
600 Rinehart Road
Lake Mary, Florida 32746
www.charismahouse.com

Cover design by Lisa Rae McClure
Design Director: Justin Evans
Instructional Designer: Regine Jean-Baptiste/!Impact Course Developers

Clipart provided by Freepik.

Visit the author's website at www.michellemcclainwalters.com.

Library of Congress Control Number: 2017935668
International Standard Book Number: 978-1-62999-452-9
E-book ISBN: 978-1-62999-453-6

17 18 19 20 21 — 9 8 7 6 5 4 3 2 1
Printed in the United States of America

In loving memory of

Tiajuana O. McClain
October 14, 1946–May 14, 1970

Mom, thank you for the ultimate
gift of life. Your mother's heart and
soldier's strength pressed through all
opposition to birth me in the earth.
Your life and legacy epitomized the
Deborah anointing. I pray that my
life has brought you great joy. I can't
wait to officially meet you in heaven!

CONTENTS

INTRODUCTION

Ye have not chosen me, but I have chosen you, and
ordained you, that ye should go and bring forth fruit,
and that your fruit should remain: that whatsoever ye
shall ask of the Father in my name, he may give it you.

—JOHN 15:16, KJV

In a world where people are looking for purpose, wandering
anxiously and aimlessly about, desperately seeking security and
significance, God is awakening in individuals an inner desire to
know His calling and destiny for their lives. This divine calling
is first birthed out of conviction. God miraculously does a work,
immediately or progressively, in a person's heart, and that work
becomes the catalyst that propels the person into action.

That is what we see happening today. The Spirit of God is
calling a remnant to abandon this culture of self-absorption,
self-gratification, and self-indulgence and embrace a lifestyle
motivated by the calling of God. It is important to know
that all Christians, whether or not they have leadership titles,
have specific callings on their lives. But in the pages of this
study guide I want to focus on a particular group whom God
is calling.

I believe that at the forefront of the next great awakening
will be women. God has a strategic plan for revival and refor-
mation in which women will play a vital role. We are living in a

time when God is calling and working through women to fulfill His redemptive plans for mankind. God is empowering and equipping women with courage and determination to find their calling and assignment to help fulfill the Great Commission to go throughout the world and make disciples. Our all-powerful God is calling ordinary women to His extraordinary work. Women will be a sign and wonder to this generation of the greatness and redeeming love of God.

The Holy Spirit is empowering women to be deliverers who do great exploits and fulfill God's purposes in the earth. Each woman's assignment is unique, but one aspect remains the same, and that is her mission to partner with God to destroy the works of the devil and set captives free. Genesis 3:15 says, "I will put enmity between you and the woman." Enmity means war, hostility, and deep-rooted hatred. The battle lines are being drawn, and there is a roar coming out of Zion that is feminine, strong, and full of compassion. This roar is coming from women anointed by God with the Holy Ghost and power to confront the powers of darkness. God is extending a great invitation to women to be part of His story that affects history.

In this hour the Lord is stirring the hearts of women to find their purpose in Him. Women are realizing that it's not about God's being part of their story; it's about their being part of His story. It's not about who is for women or against them; it's about whom women are for. Women don't just have authority; they are living under the authority of the One who has all power.

Let us make no mistake; embracing the marvelous calling of God is neither easy nor glamorous. There will always be obstacles to overcome and seemingly more attractive ways to live. Yet God calls us to live as His ambassadors among the nations to spread His love and make an eternal difference among those in our sphere of influence.

SWEET WISDOM

It's not about God's being part of my story; it's about my being part of God's story. It's not about who is for me or against me; it's about whom I am for. I don't just have authority; I am living under the authority of the One who has all power.

The world is hungrier than ever for more women to step up and break through the glass cage that limits their influence in the world. Women must prepare to step up to the leadership plate and dare to do more, be more, and give more. Only when we stop cowering to our fear of not being "enough" and start owning the power that resides within each of us to affect change can the millions of women less fortunate than us—women who are living with little hope or opportunity—ever exercise their power. It is not just our *responsibility* as women to become more courageous in how we live and lead; it's our obligation.

The Deborah Anointing Study Guide is designed to help you walk in the awesome responsibility and call of God to live and lead boldly. Using the companion video teachings, *The Deborah Anointing* book, and this workbook for group or individual study, you will gain the tools and techniques you need to embrace the call to be a woman of power and influence. You will be challenged as you watch the video recordings (which are availble at www.michellemcclainbooks.com), read the book, and answer the lesson questions. Whether you are embarking on this journey to embrace the anointing of Deborah in a group or on your own, you can be confident that this material will equip you to walk boldly in your God-given calling to live and lead.

GETTING STARTED

To everything there is a season, a time for every purpose
under heaven.

—ECCLESIASTES 3:1

The Deborah Anointing Study Guide and video recordings are
companions to *The Deborah Anointing* book. As inspiring as
the book is, once the reality of everyday life sets in, it's easy to
let distractions drown out the conviction we may feel from the
readings. This study guide will fill in that gap and show you
how to apply the principles from Deborah's life and leadership
to your own.

Working through the material in a small-group setting will
help provide accountability and shed deeper insight into the
lessons as members share what God has taught them during
their individual study. My prayer is that you will approach
each lesson in this study guide prayerfully. Open your heart
to the truth of God's Word as you watch the videos, which are
available at www.michellemcclainbooks.com. Meditate on the
scriptures presented in each corresponding chapter of the book,
and honestly examine your heart. Push yourself not only to
build a plan of action but also to apply it to your everyday life.
Arise as Deborah did, and embrace your call. The world awaits
the full manifestation of your destiny.

LESSON OUTLINE

The lessons within this study guide are designed to help you embrace and grow into the traits that characterize a woman who possesses the Deborah anointing so you can live and lead as a modern-day Deborah. The reflection questions for small-group discussion follow the corresponding video teaching. At the end of each section of study you will be prompted to devise an action plan to implement and practice the concepts within the lesson.

Deborah's name means "bee," and that is key to understanding her anointing and navigating through this study guide. She was as sweet as a honeybee. While wasps are naturally aggressive, honeybees understand their function, are focused on their leader, serve their colonies, and reproduce. Honeybees are extremely knowledgeable and consistently work their plan to produce sweet honey, which leaves a legacy for generations to come.

In the same manner, the *Deborah Anointing* book, study guide, and video teaching will empower you to gain confidence in your calling, understand the power of worship, become a servant leader, and reproduce. The workbook has a honeybee theme to help you embrace and grow into a woman of wisdom and discernment. The "Bee Informed" sections will help you become extremely knowledgeable in the concepts of the lesson. And the "Worker Bee Plan" sections will help you develop practical steps to apply the wisdom you gain in study.

Also, remember, the foundation of each lesson is built on the corresponding video teaching, so always watch the video teaching before you start the workbook lesson. After you watch the teaching, work through the questions in the study guide to enhance your learning.

TIPS FOR PERSONAL STUDY

Here are some suggestions to help you engage in individual study:

- ◆ Always begin your time of study with prayer. Ask God to help you understand and apply the concepts in your life.

- ◆ Read and reread the passage(s) of Scripture. The Word of God is foundational, and understanding the Scriptures will help you apply the concepts consistently.

- ◆ Write your answers in the spaces provided in the workbook. Writing down your answers will help you express your understanding of the concepts clearly.

TIPS FOR GROUP STUDY

If you are using this workbook as part of a group study, here are some suggestions to help you get the most out of the material:

- ◆ Be prepared. Spend some time in preparation before each session. Your planning will enhance class discussions.

- ◆ Participate in the group. Be willing to discuss what you have learned from the video recordings, book chapters, and workbook lessons, and encourage the others in your group to do the same. Share what God has taught you, but do not dominate the time or lecture the group.

+ Listen attentively. Encourage silent and hesitant group members to participate in the discussion. Give words of affirmation whenever possible.

+ Explore all options within the materials. Use the biblical passages in the lessons or information within *The Deborah Anointing* book rather than outside authorities for group discussion. This will help group members deepen their understanding of the material presented in the workbook teachings.

If you are facilitating a group, visit www.michellemcclain books.com to download a copy of *The Deborah Anointing Leader's Guide*, which contains tips, templates, and lesson plans for running a group study.

Lesson 1

PROCESS THE CALL

Village life ceased. It ceased until I, Deborah, arose; I arose like a mother in Israel.

—Judges 5:7

In this lesson you will:

+ Identify the calling and keys of the Deborah anointing
+ Explain the time and seasons of the call

Read the introduction and chapter 1 of *The Deborah Anointing*.

God is awakening women to arise and take the dominion He gave them in the beginning. He is awakening them to a purpose greater than themselves. Many women in the body of Christ have been trapped in tradition and locked into captivity by cultural and gender prejudices. Yet God is empowering women to break through barriers and overcome obstacles set up to derail them from their God-given destiny. God is anointing women to be co-laborers with Him and with men in redeeming and restoring humanity and the earth.

This is a season in which the Holy Spirit is raising women

up to positions of leadership and creating a desire in them to discover and embrace the fullness of their purpose on earth. The word *embrace* means to "accept or support (a belief, theory, or change) willingly and enthusiastically."[1] God is destroying belief systems that hinder and cripple women in their calling. God also is enlightening the eyes of many men to understand the call and purpose of women. This understanding will cause men to train, equip, support, and make room for women to minister beside them in the battle for the souls of humanity.

Women are being released to minister in power as they live in the fullness of the Spirit. Women are being used in extraordinary ways to impact and influence the world around them. God is equipping women to be agents of healing and deliverance to those in their sphere of influence. God not only is setting women free from years of bondage and torment but also is empowering them to set other women free.

Jesus set women free to be beautiful and powerful people who exemplify the beauty and diversity of God. Women are so diverse in their strengths that it is simply impossible to explain the grace that flows from their lives. But the Bible always leaves us with an example and pattern to follow.

Deborah the prophetess and judge is that example. Deborah governed God's people with a mother's heart, a soldier's strength, and a firm resolve. She received her marching orders from the King of Glory to bring healing and deliverance to her generation. Deborah was living in a time when the people of Israel were suffering from the consequences of their disobedience to God. There was a great vacancy of the presence of God in the land. Amid these circumstances Deborah was called to become the spokeswoman for God, a divine commission that would lead the nation to victory.

BEE INFORMED *If you have not done so already, take time to watch the lesson 1 video, "Process the Call." Use the space below to take notes.*

aWAKE - God wants to awaken us to our purpose
Arise / Advance in New Territories
If u wants to advance you will
ABORTION IS A PERVERSION

ARISE IN CONFIDENCE

Woman of God, the Lord is extending an invitation to you to arise and become a modern-day Deborah. Embracing this marvelous call requires that you take time to discover the traits and characteristics of Deborah, who was a woman of influence, conviction, and power. It also requires you to process how God desires to manifest this calling in your life. But whether you are leading in business, religion, family, arts and entertainment, government, education, or media, you can be a modern-day Deborah.

As a modern-day Deborah, you are called to be confident in yourself, your gifts, and your anointing.

How confident are you in yourself? Provide examples to support your answer.

_____

_____

_____

3

Take a moment to evaluate your self-confidence using the following assessment. Read each statement, and rate how the description best characterizes you. Circle a number from one to five, with one representing not at all and five representing very often. As you rate the statement, select the first option that comes to mind, not the one that describes who you wish you could be. This is not a pass-or-fail test. The goal of this assessment is to help you be more aware of your level of self-confidence.

	Not at All	Rarely	Sometimes	Often	Very Often
I handle new situations with relative comfort and ease.	1	2	(3)	4	5
I keep trying, even after others have given up.	1	2	3	(4)	5
I feel positive and am energized about my life.	1	2	3	(4)	5
If a particular task looks too difficult, I will avoid doing it.	1	2	(3)	4	5
I like to connect with people who I consider to be successful.	1	2	(3)	4	5

	Not at All	Rarely	Sometimes	Often	Very Often
I achieve the goals I set for myself.	1	2	(3)	4	5
I need to experience success early in a process, or else I will not continue.	1	2	3	(4)	5
When I face difficulties, I feel hopeless and negative.	1	2	(3)	4	5
When I overcome an obstacle, I think about the lessons I've learned.	1	2	3	4	(5)
I relate the most to people who work very hard and still don't accomplish their goals.	(1)	2	3	4	5
If I work hard to solve a problem, I'll find the answer.	1	2	3	(4)	5
I receive positive feedback on my work and achievements.	1	(2)	3	4	5

	Not at All	Rarely	Sometimes	Often	Very Often
I believe that if I work hard, I will achieve my goals.	1	2	3	(4)	5

When you complete the assessment, calculate your totals. Add the numbers together that you circled in each row.

Total Self-Confidence Score: _____

Read and circle the self-confidence level that matches your total self-confidence score.

+ **Graced to Arise** (up to 25)
    Gratitude must be a big focal point for those seeking to embrace the confidence of a Deborah. Instead of focusing on what you do not have, take time to be grateful to God for the things you have achieved in your life.

+ **Growing Power Broker** (26–45) (43)
    You are a woman of power and influence, and you are starting to recognize these God-given skills and abilities within yourself. Now it is time for you to stop being hard on yourself and start building on your strengths.

+ **Emerging Influencer** (46 and up)
    You are emerging with the confidence to live and lead like a Deborah. Continue learning from your experiences and nurturing your self-confidence.

What did the assessment results reveal about you? Were the assessment results expected or surprising to you?

_____

_____

_____

List some ways you can continue to grow in your self-confidence.

_____

_____

_____

WORKER BEE PLAN

Select one of the strategies you listed for growing in self-confidence, and practice using this technique within the next week to boost your self-confidence. Journal your experience below, and record ways you can continue this practice in the future.

_____

_____

_____

_____

_____

_____

CONFIDENTLY GIFTED

Deborah was gifted with many skills and abilities. Her confidence in her God-given abilities allowed her to ultimately use her gifts to save a whole nation. Modern-day Deborahs must assess their gifts and learn to confidently deploy these gifts on behalf of the kingdom of God to see God's people blessed and living the life God designed for them.

Take an inventory of the various skills and abilities God has given you. Make a list of these gifts. Consider your technical, transferable, and personal skills when creating your list.

Technical skills are the specialized skills and knowledge required to perform specific duties, sometimes referred to as "work skills." Transferable skills are the ones required to perform a variety of tasks. They can be transferred from one area to another. Personal skills are the individual attributes you have, such as personality traits and work habits.

My technical skills	My transferable skills	My personal skills

Read James 1:17. According to this verse, who is the source of your skills and abilities?

_____

_____

_____

Every good and perfect gift comes from God. Your abilities and gifts are given to you from God.

How confident are you in using your skills listed previously for the kingdom of God? How have you used some of these skills in the past to advance the kingdom of God?

_____

_____

_____

Are your gifts and abilities surrendered to the Lord for Him to call upon and use at any particular time?

_____

_____

_____

How do you go about surrendering your gifts and skills to the Lord?

_____

_____

_____

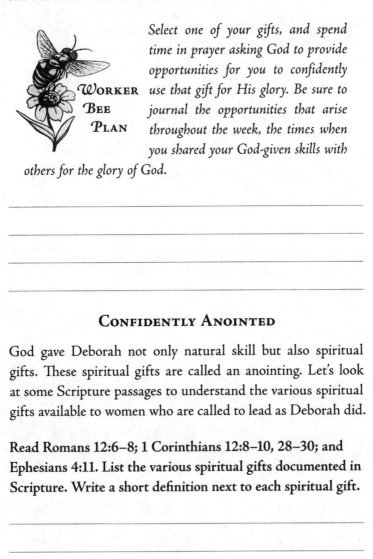

Select one of your gifts, and spend time in prayer asking God to provide opportunities for you to confidently **WORKER** *use that gift for His glory. Be sure to* **BEE** *journal the opportunities that arise* **PLAN** *throughout the week, the times when you shared your God-given skills with others for the glory of God.*

_____

_____

_____

_____

CONFIDENTLY ANOINTED

God gave Deborah not only natural skill but also spiritual gifts. These spiritual gifts are called an anointing. Let's look at some Scripture passages to understand the various spiritual gifts available to women who are called to lead as Deborah did.

Read Romans 12:6–8; 1 Corinthians 12:8–10, 28–30; and Ephesians 4:11. List the various spiritual gifts documented in Scripture. Write a short definition next to each spiritual gift.

_____

_____

_____

_____

_____

_____

What do you believe God has anointed you to do? Circle the gifts in the list from the previous question that you believe God has graced you with. In the space below describe some of the experiences you have had using these gifts.

_____

_____

_____

Deborah also had the spiritual gifts of administration, knowledge, and apostleship. Modern-day Deborahs possess the spiritual gifts of leadership, discernment, mercy, evangelism, working of miracles, exhortation, pastoring and shepherding, faith, prophecy, giving, serving/ministering, healing, teaching, interpretation of tongues, gifts of tongues, and wisdom. Yet the anointing of Deborah is not to be used just in the church. Deborah deployed her anointing to help the army of Israel, at her home, and when she was judging cases while sitting under her palm tree.

WORKER BEE PLAN

Do you confidently use the anointing God has given you in all your spheres of influence (work, home, church, and so on)? Why or why not? Provide some examples of how you can engage your spiritual gifts in different spheres.

_____

_____

_____

_____

CALLED TO ARISE

In Judges 5:7 Deborah not only answered the call to live and lead Israel courageously; she also answered the call to confidently arise. The call to arise was for her to confidently take her proper place as a woman filled with God's power. In accepting the call to be a modern-day Deborah, you must understand the process of the call and realize that God has called you to arise in power, in hostility, to be a voice, to establish, and to pioneer.

Use the introduction of *The Deborah Anointing* to define the leadership qualities a modern-day Deborah must possess and perfect to disciple the next generation and walk fully in her call.

+ Arise in power

_____

_____

+ Arise in hostility

_____

_____

+ Arise to be a voice

_____

_____

+ Arise to establish

_____

_____

+ Arise to pioneer

_____

_____

Deborah's power comes from the Holy Spirit. The Holy Spirit makes gifts of faith, healing, and miracles accessible to modern-day Deborahs so they can be bold leaders.

Are you currently using any of the power gifts made accessible to you through the Holy Spirit?

_____

_____

_____

Which of the power gifts are you interested in developing in your life? Why?

_____

_____

_____

List some intentional steps you can take to grow in the gifts of faith, healing, and miracles.

_____

_____

_____

The ability to arise and confront the kingdom of the enemy is part of the Deborah anointing. Modern-day Deborahs are often called to confidently arise amid hostility to challenge the powers of darkness around them.

What are some causes within your family, community, and nation, and within the world that require courageous leaders to arise, confront evil powers, and lead people into God's freedom?

_____

_____

_____

How is God calling and equipping you to arise and liberate the people of this cause?

_____

_____

_____

Deborah confidently arose to lend her voice to the voiceless.

Are you willing to arise and lend your voice to the cause you identified with both your words and your deeds?

_____

_____

_____

Modern-day Deborahs are called to establish the kingdom of God here on earth. Deborah did this by standing boldly in the call of God.

Take a moment and think through some of the past trials you have had to endure. What lessons learned from those trials are empowering you to be persistent and resilient today?

_____

_____

_____

Read 1 Peter 5:10. What does God promise to those who are willing to be established in the bold calling of the Lord despite trials and hardships?

_____

_____

_____

Deborah was a pioneer. She was a woman living in a male-dominated society, leading the charge to disciple the next generation.

In what ways are you pioneering in your family or community?

_____

_____

_____

What does it feel like to pioneer something that will have implications for generations to come?

_____

_____

_____

SWEET WISDOM

Modern-day Deborahs will be women after God's heart who will lead a generation to stand for God's ways of righteousness.

There is a divine urgency for modern-day Deborahs to arise confidently in power, to give a voice to the voiceless by challenging and destroying the powers of darkness, and to establish the kingdom of God here on earth.

Read Isaiah 32:17. According to this verse, where do we find confidence to lead?

_____

_____

_____

Deborah received the confidence to lead not from her righteousness but from the righteousness of Christ.

WORKER BEE PLAN

Spend time in prayer asking God to give you confidence in Christ's righteousness so that you will walk in boldness. Use the closing prayer on pages 7–8 of The Deborah Anointing *as you arise and awake to new levels of confidence in Christ.*

POSSESS THE KEYS

Embracing the Deborah anointing calls for increased confidence in yourself, your gifts, and your anointing, and for you to arise boldly to possess the keys of the anointing. The keys to activating the Deborah anointing in your life are found in strategic intercession, judging, prophecy, mothering, developing military strategy, agitating, and worshipping.

Define the keys of Deborah's anointing using notes from the video recording and *The Deborah Anointing* book.

1. Strategic intercession

_____

_____

_____

2. Judging

_____

_____

_____

_____

3. Prophecy

_____

_____

_____

4. Mothering

_____

_____

_____

5. Developing military strategy

_____

_____

_____

6. Agitating

_____

_____

_____

7. Worshipping

_____

_____

_____

Place a check mark next to the key(s) of the Deborah anointing in which you feel most confident.

_____ Strategic intercession

_____ Judging

_____ Prophecy

_____ Mothering

_____ Developing military strategy

__X__ Agitating

_____ Worshipping

Note some ways you see the keys of Deborah's anointing operating in your life.

_____

_____

_____

_____

_____

_____

_____

_____

What are the hindrances keeping you from possessing all the keys of Deborah's anointing?

_____

_____

_____

_____

_____

_____

Deborah and a host of other biblical characters serve as testimonies of what happens when we place our confidence in Christ. These faithful witnesses serve as reminders that we must not allow anything to hinder us from living in the calling to be modern-day Deborahs.

WORKER BEE PLAN

Identify something you can do today to cast off the hindrances that keep you from fully possessing the Deborah anointing in your life, ministry, and/ or career.

_____

_____

_____

_____

_____

BEE INFORMED *If you have not done so already, return to the video to watch the conclusion of lesson 1, "Process the Call." Use the space below to take notes.*

_____

_____

_____

_____

_____

_____

_____

SEASONS OF THE CALL

Galatians 6:9 tells us, "And let us not be weary in well doing: for in due season we shall reap, if we faint not" (KJV). The Deborah anointing is a powerful mandate for women who were born to lead and influence a generation to the righteousness and purity found in Jesus Christ. Embracing every aspect of the Deborah anointing will consume many seasons of your life as you nurture your confidence, mature in your gifts and anointing, walk in boldness, and deploy your God-given authority to change and transform the world.

As you develop the various aspects of the call to be a modern-day Deborah, there is also a process God is working within you to sustain the call. Just as there are multiple seasons of the year, the process to sustain your calling to be a Deborah will require multiple spiritual seasons of maturing and perfecting.

The ability to discern the season you are currently in is

extremely important to maximizing your call to boldly lead in the kingdom of God as a Deborah.

Read Judges 4:14–17. How did Deborah's ability to discern the time help Barak?

_____

_____

_____

Deborah's ability to know the time helped to deliver God's people out of years of bondage. In Scripture the word *time* can mean an opportunity, appointed season, day, or measure of time, sequence, or duration.[2] Deborah's ability in Judges 4:14 to discern the season and articulate "for this is the day" helped her to take hold of the opportunity God provided on that given day to save the nation of Israel.

In all seasons of the call, to truly embrace the Deborah anointing, modern-day women must seek God to discern and devise a plan for their current spiritual season. God has specific instructions and opportunities tied to your current season to help you lead boldly in the kingdom of God.

Considering the different seasons shared in the first chapter of *The Deborah Anointing* and in the video, what season are you currently experiencing as you embrace the Deborah anointing? What evidence or experiences point to this particular season?

_____

_____

_____

Build a plan for success in your current season by using the following assessment. Read the following statements. Place a check mark next to five statements that best describe how you feel about your life today. Please check the items that best identify how you currently feel about your life, not how you would like to feel.

☐ 1. I've been feeling uncomfortable with myself and my calling lately.

☑ 2. I feel as if I am just coming out of a very hard season and my life is starting to come together for the better.

☐ 3. I feel a balance between times of natural spiritual growth and times of stillness.

☐ 4. I see tremendous evidence of my hard work over the seasons.

☐ 5. I have a great balance of work and play in my life.

☐ 6. I feel as if my dreams are dying, and I am just not sure what the next steps are for me.

☐ 7. I am currently living in the overflow, harvesting and storing up.

☑ 8. I am starting to develop a new confidence in God to help me accomplish things I could never accomplish before on my own.

☒ 9. I am implementing new revelation that I am receiving from the Lord and slowly seeing fruit.

☐ 10. I am feeling unfruitful; I do a lot but don't necessarily see fruit from all my labor.

☒ 11. I am filled with anticipation for all the rewards God has for me in this season of life.

☐ 12. It feels as if I am being crushed. The pressure in both my personal and professional life is too much. Life seems to have crashed in on me all at once.

☒ 13. Confidence in my abilities is growing, and I am more confident in God's abilities in me.

☐ 14. I am celebrating the abundance of God that I have seen manifesting for me in this season.

☒ 15. I am experiencing great times of wisdom and revelation as God is helping me understand specifics about my call.

☐ 16. I am confident in God and God's ability within me to change the world around me.

Each of the five statements you selected represents a season. On the evaluation key, circle the number next to the statement you selected. For example, if you selected statement number two, in the evaluation key, circle "2. Spring." The season with the most circles in the evaluation key marks your current season.

EVALUATION KEY:

1. Winter	5. Summer	9. Spring	13. Spring
2. Spring	6. Winter	10. Winter	14. Fall
3. Summer	7. Fall	11. Fall	15. Summer
4. Fall	8. Spring	12. Winter	16. Summer

My season is ___WINTER_____.

Did your assessment reflect the season you feel you are experiencing? Why or why not?

_____

_____

_____

Now that you have identified and verified your current season, it is time to build a plan. Find the plan that matches your assessment results. Use the questions in the plan to design a successful strategy to help you garner everything God desires for you during this season of your life.

+ Winter season plan

+ Spring season plan

+ Summer season plan

+ Fall season plan

MY WINTER SEASON PLAN

+ **Characteristic:** Feeling cold, uncomfortable, and as if you are in a wilderness

25

- ✦ **Strategy:** Reflect and meditate, asking the Holy Spirit a lot of questions. This is also a time of measurement (i.e., asking, "Who are You, Lord? What do You want me to do?").

Describe your winter season.

_____

_____

_____

_____

Spend time meditating on Hosea 2:14. Write a prayer asking God for greater insight on your identity and your calling.

_____

_____

_____

_____

What has been your greatest lesson learned during this season?

_____

_____

_____

_____

What aspects of your relationship with God have changed in this season?

_____

_____

_____

_____

How has God shaped your identity in this season?

_____

_____

_____

_____

What instruction has God shared with you concerning your destiny?

_____

_____

_____

_____

WORKER
BEE
PLAN

Spend time in reflection this week, and journal about the goodness of God. Write a list of forty times when God has demonstrated His faithfulness in your life. Close out your time of reflection with a prayer of thanksgiving.

_____

_____

_____

_____

_____

_____

MY SPRING SEASON PLAN

+ **Characteristic:** A time to implement the instructions and new revelations you received during your winter season

+ **Strategy:** Develop new confidence, and strengthen new connections.

Describe your spring season.

_____

_____

_____

What has God called you to carry out in this season? How are you implementing God's instructions?

_____

_____

_____

In what ways have you been stagnant or neutral about pursuing the purpose of God for your life? What is required of you to change this position of stagnation or neutrality?

_____

_____

_____

What do you need to live in the fullness of your destiny and purpose?

_____

_____

_____

What types of training could you gain to help you successfully achieve your God-given destiny?

_____

_____

_____

What is hindering you from living in your destiny?

_____

_____

_____

_____

WORKER BEE PLAN

God desires to deliver us from every hindrance. Therefore we must purpose in our hearts to believe that God can deliver us from every stronghold. Spend time praying and asking God for a desire to be delivered from strongholds and to align you for your assignment by bringing forth new connections and mentors. Use the space provided to write any insights the Lord gives you.

_____

_____

_____

_____

_____

_____

_____

_____

_____

My summer season plan

- **Characteristic**: Everything seems to come to life.

- **Strategy**: Increase the levels of worship, prayer, and reading of the Word of God.

Describe your summer season.

_____

_____

_____

_____

How are you growing in your relationship with Jesus?

_____

_____

_____

How have you been able to achieve balance in your life?

_____

_____

_____

_____

Provide an example of how God has helped you achieve greater balance in your life.

_____

_____

_____

_____

_____

How would you describe your level of confidence in your assignment?

_____

_____

_____

_____

What details or blueprints has God revealed to you during this season to help you understand your call?

_____

_____

_____

_____

WORKER BEE PLAN

Greater balance and more understanding are achieved during the summer season by deepening our intimacy with God. In the upcoming week increase your level of relational intimacy with God through worship, prayer, and reading the Word of God. Journal the results of increasing your times of prayer, worship, and Bible reading.

_____

_____

_____

_____

_____

_____

MY FALL SEASON PLAN

+ **Characteristic:** Filled with anticipation and reaping a harvest

+ **Strategy:** Posture yourself in humility and thanksgiving.

Describe your fall season.

_____

_____

_____

How does it feel to see evidence of your hard work throughout the seasons?

_____

_____

_____

What is your plan for harvesting and storing up wisdom and resources in this season?

_____

_____

_____

How have you stopped and celebrated the abundance God has brought you into this season?

_____

_____

_____

What are the best lessons you have learned from submitting yourself to the sacrificial demands of God's call?

_____

_____

_____

Read Galatians 6:9. Reflect and journal on the role of obedience in past seasons and how surrendering to God has contributed to your current season of harvest.

_____

_____

_____

_____

WORKER BEE PLAN

In the fall season of life God must be actively engaged in every detail of our lives. Write a prayer to encourage your active pursuit of God in this season and to activate the power of the Holy Spirit in every detail of your life.

_____

_____

_____

_____

_____

Lesson 2

THE POWER OF WORSHIP

Then sang Deborah and Barak son of Abinoam on that day, saying, for the leaders who took the lead in Israel, for the people who offered themselves willingly, bless the Lord! Hear, O kings; give ear, O princes; I will sing to the Lord. I will sing praise to the Lord, the God of Israel.

—JUDGES 5:1–3, AMPC

In this lesson you will summarize the benefit of developing in the areas of worship and prayer to sustain your calling and anointing.

Read chapter 4 of *The Deborah Anointing*.

Deborah was a worshipper. She loved the Lord with all her heart, mind, soul, and strength. Similarly it is from times of worship that modern-day women draw the confidence to live out their calling to transform the world to the glory of God. True worship will always bring us balance and resolve because in the presence of the Lord we learn how to see life from God's perspective. Deborah was a worshipping warrior who had

God's perspective. She learned to love what God loved and hate His enemies.

Modern-day Deborahs must seek to find balance as they live out their assignment and calling. There will be times as you embrace your calling when the enemy will try to fill your heart with fear. This happens to many women. They are plagued with the fear of not being good enough to fulfill all the demands of life and their call. Yet during times of worship when we are in the presence of the Lord, the truth of God's love and strength will destroy our fears.

One of the greatest monsters I wrestled with in my leadership was a lack of confidence in the calling and gifting God had for me. I battled insecurity, fear, and the obsessive need to compare myself with others. Comparison and competition are enemies of the call of God. These were enemies to my confidence that tried to get the best of me. We usually take our weaknesses and compare them with someone else's strengths, which only causes us to become more insecure and fearful.

The only thing that can cast out the spirit of fear is the love of God—and worship is the place where love is perfected and peace of mind is restored. Scripture tells us that "perfect love casts out fear" for "there is no fear in love" (1 John 4:18). Woman of God, we must learn to worship God, and out of that place of worship God can calm our fears and insecurities and empower us to lead with confidence.

If you have not done so already, take time to watch lesson 2, "The Power of Worship." Use the space below to take notes.

_____

_____

_____

_____

_____

_____

_____

_____

ACCESSING THE PRESENCE OF THE LORD

The ability to access the presence of the Lord affords us the opportunity to become effective leaders and to change a generation. In the presence of the Lord, Deborah was able to achieve everything God commissioned her to accomplish. Modern-day Deborahs must also access the power available in the presence of the Lord to walk in the fullness of their destiny and purpose.

Read Matthew 5:8. What is the presence of the Lord, according to this verse?

_____

_____

_____

Read Jeremiah 29:13. According to this scripture, how do we access the presence of the Lord?

_____

_____

_____

_____

_____

Worship and prayer are instrumental in bringing us into the presence of God, where our call is cultivated.

How would you define *worship*? Use Scripture and other biblical resources to support your definition.

_____

_____

_____

_____

_____

Worship is the Greek word *proskuneō*, which means to express respect or reverence.[1] Therefore worship is based on our frame of heart and our attitude toward God. Worship brings us into the presence of God. And it is there in God's presence that we draw our confidence to fight and that we are prepared, as Deborah was, for war.

WORKER BEE PLAN

Consider some ways you can make worship part of every moment of your day. What steps and practices would you need to implement to deepen your level of worship and spend more time in God's presence? Throughout the next week increase your time in worship. Journal any benefits you received from implementing those steps to become more consistent in worship.

HINDRANCES TO THE PRESENCE OF GOD

As was previously mentioned, one of the biggest enemies to accessing the presence of the Lord and walking in the calling of God is fear. Fear comes in many different shapes and sizes. But according to Proverbs 29:25, fear has one goal, which is to ensnare you and to keep you tangled so you do not fulfill your destiny. For example, fear seeks to ensnare you through anxiety, fear of people's opinions and thoughts, fear of failure, and even fear of success.

Name your greatest fear. How is this fear keeping you from moving into your calling?

Think back to the first time you experienced this fear. What were the circumstances?

_____

_____

_____

What situations or circumstances make you most fearful about your calling?

_____

_____

_____

Read 1 John 4:16–18. Write your interpretation of this passage of Scripture.

_____

_____

_____

What is the remedy for fear?

_____

_____

_____

The love of God is the only thing that can destroy the spirit of fear. Deborah teaches us that there is only one way to deal with the spirit of fear, and that is to dwell in the presence of the Lord in worship. Worship is the place where love is perfected and peace of mind is restored. Deborah could move in courage and defeat her enemies because she was filled with God's love for herself and for the people of Israel!

Worship is the place where love is perfected and peace of mind is restored.

Be intentional about being filled with God's love. How can you make knowing the love of God a daily pursuit? In the space provided, detail your schedule for the next week, and identify something you can do each day to become more aware of God's love for you. What would your schedule look like if you sought to recognize God's love for you every hour of your day?

_____

_____

_____

_____

_____

_____

_____

_____

BEE INFORMED *If you have not done so already, return to the video teaching to watch the conclusion of lesson 2, "The Power of Worship." Use the space below to take notes.*

_____

_____

_____

_____

_____

_____

_____

_____

BENEFITS OF WORSHIP

Modern-day Deborahs must cultivate a lifestyle of praise and worship before operating in the Deborah anointing. Worship honors God and brings benefits to the worshipper.

Read the following Scripture passages, and record the benefit(s) God bestows upon the worshipper.

+ Exodus 20:3–7:

_____

_____

_____

+ Psalm 34:4:

_____

_____

_____

+ Psalm 91:1:

_____

_____

_____

+ Ecclesiastes 3:1–8:

_____

_____

_____

+ Isaiah 32:17:

_____

_____

_____

Scripture reminds us that God gives special advantages to those who cultivate a heart of worship. We as modern-day Deborahs can be confident that engaging in worship aids in building our relationship with God by:

1. Giving us a perspective and language to communicate with God

2. Helping us understand our identity

3. Destroying our fears

4. Bringing balance to our lives

5. Producing confidence in us to see breakthrough

WORKER BEE PLAN

God desires to provide us with everything we need to fulfill our call. As we worship Him, we receive benefits from the Lord that empower us to further live in our divine purpose. Journal about moments in the past when you have seen the benefits of worship in your life.

_____

_____

_____

_____

_____

_____

_____

_____

What are some ways you can be more intentional in your worship? During the next week, apply some of the practical steps you listed to help you become an intentional worshipper.

Journal the outcomes and benefits you received throughout the week as you engaged in times of intentional worship.

_____

_____

_____

_____

_____

_____

BREAKTHROUGH IN WORSHIP

The key to seeing the benefits of worship is to dwell in the presence of the Lord. In the presence of the Lord there is breakthrough to fulfill God's calling for your life. There is also breakthrough to live in the fullness of the destiny and purpose God has designed for your life. Since God is the same yesterday, today, and forever, we can be assured that the same Lord who provided breakthrough for others in the past desires to do the same for you.

When we experience breakthrough in worship and prayer, God's power is released to bring victory to our circumstances. As we engage in worship and prayer that brings forth breakthrough, everything that seemed impossible will be made possible through Christ Jesus. Experiencing breakthrough in prayer and worship helps us also to break free from the resistance of the enemy and to embrace God's will. There are four specific realms of breakthrough the Lord wants to bring in our lives through prayer and worship.

PERSONAL BREAKTHROUGH

Read Luke 22:39–46. The Mount of Olives is a picture of God providing a personal breakthrough. How would you define a personal breakthrough? Use Luke 22:39–46 to support your definition.

_____

_____

_____

_____

_____

_____

There are barriers and gates governed by demonic forces. These barriers and gates are made accessible to our enemy through our sins. When demonic forces access these open places in our lives, they are at work seeking to secure our defeat. Therefore every believer has the responsibility to seek breakthrough in prayer and worship to overthrow the enemy's strategy. We can confidently seek God for the victory because Jesus has a plan for us to prosper and succeed. It is in prayer and worship that we gain access to these plans that allow us to overcome the evil tactics of the enemy. We can rest assured that in the presence of the Lord we will receive personal breakthrough and the wisdom to overcome every evil force in our lives.

Corporate Breakthrough

Read Acts 1. The upper room encounter is a demonstration of a corporate breakthrough. According to this passage, how would you define a corporate breakthrough?

_____

_____

_____

Corporate breakthrough comes as a group of believers relentlessly pursues God's presence. Every local church must develop a desire to see corporate breakthrough during its times of prayer and worship. Having a culture of corporate breakthrough will enable the church to sustain growth while pursuing the purposes of God for its community, its nation, and the world. Modern-day Deborahs are called to arise and lead the charge for corporate breakthrough within their churches. They must arise because when the body of Christ does not stand up and believe God for corporate breakthrough, the enemy determines our destiny and the future of our region.

Territorial Breakthrough

Read Acts 8. In the story of Simon the sorcerer we see God providing a territorial breakthrough. Use the passage from Acts 8 to define a territorial breakthrough.

_____

_____

_____

God desires to use you to transform the world through your sphere of influence. Your sphere of influence, which you govern, is known as a territory. The powers of darkness and the enemies of God do not want you to gain authority in prayer and worship because whole territories and people groups can be saved through your influence. Therefore modern-day Deborahs must arise and inspire others to seek God for a territorial breakthrough to overcome the challenges within their region. When Deborah arose and pursued the Lord for her territory, the whole nation of Israel gained victory over its enemies. In the same manner, when women arise in prayer and worship, they will see a divine victory over the enemies of their communities.

Generational Breakthrough

Read Numbers 14:24. This Old Testament passage presents a generational breakthrough. How would you define a generational breakthrough?

_____

_____

_____

Generational breakthrough is when a whole generation is able to advance into its God-given inheritance. This type of breakthrough is also visible in the generation of Joshua and Caleb. Their pursuit of God enabled a whole generation to reap the abundant spoils of God's promise. Under Deborah's leadership all the generations living in Israel were freed from bondage and gained their God-given inheritance of rulership. Thus, the modern-day Deborah's pursuit of the presence of

God through worship is not just personal; it is for the benefit of generations to come.

WORKER BEE PLAN

The benefit of worship is break-through in our lives. Consider the various types of breakthrough we gain in worship. Which type of breakthrough do you desire most? Spend time pursuing God for the heart and confidence to see this breakthrough manifest. Review chapter 9 in The Deborah Anointing, *"Deborah the Preserver," to learn more about developing a breakthrough spirit.*

PRACTICING GOD'S PRESENCE

Encountering God in a personal and transforming way was the fuel that enabled Deborah to live in the fullness of her call. She was a passionate worshipper and practiced the art of dwelling in the presence of God. Her pursuit of God gave her the confidence and breakthrough she needed to be a warrior and deliverer for her nation. Modern-day Deborahs are called to confidently lead God's people to victory in all sectors of society. To accomplish this call, our primary desire must become the presence of the Lord.

What are the steps to dwelling in the presence of the Lord? What do each of these steps accomplish? Review chapter 4 of *The Deborah Anointing*, "Deborah the Worshipping Warrior," especially pages 44 and 45.

_____

_____

_____

_____

The secret to worship is to dwell in the presence of the Lord through listening, watching, waiting, and finding. When we dwell in the presence of the Lord, we will watch God burst through everything seeking to confine us. In the secret place with God we have an opportunity to listen to God's instructions and find the strength our hearts, minds, and souls need to wait for God's promises to manifest.

1. Practice dwelling in God's presence using the listening, watching, waiting, and finding techniques. One way to apply these techniques is through Scripture meditation. This is the practice of letting the Word of God dwell in our lives. Our times of meditation should include both moments of worship and fellowship with the Lord through prayer. In the upcoming week spend time meditating on the following Scripture passages using these steps: Read the Scripture passage, and listen for the verse that resonates with you.

2. Write down the verse.

3. Repeat the verse, pondering each word. With each recitation, emphasize a different word in the verse. Meditation takes time, so be attentive as you repeat the scripture. Listen to the sounds of the words.

4. Watch for your reactions to the verses.

5. Wait for God's leading to help you find the revelation God desires to bring to you through this particular Scripture verse.

6. Journal any insight God has revealed to you about the overall process.

Meditate and journal on Psalm 16.

_____

_____

_____

_____

_____

Meditate and journal on Psalm 25.

_____

_____

_____

_____

Meditate and journal on Psalm 145.

_____

_____

_____

_____

_____

_____

Meditate and journal on Psalm 9.

_____

_____

_____

_____

_____

_____

WORKER BEE PLAN

Harp and bowl is a worship style that emphasizes building intimacy with God. This style of worship has its origins in Revelation 5:8 and incorporates both worship and prayer. During your worship and prayer time, read one of the verses that resonated with you during your meditation time. Write the verse in the space provided, and again spend time reading the verse aloud. Then begin praying the scripture by using the words of the verse as a starting point to pray. It may be easier to write out a prayer using the scripture verse and then read your prayer aloud. Also, try to sing the scripture using the tune of your favorite song.

_____

_____

_____

_____

_____

_____

_____

_____

_____

_____

_____

_____

_____

_____

_____

_____

_____

_____

_____

_____

_____

Lesson 3

BECOMING A SERVANT

How forceful are right words!

—JOB 6:25

In this lesson you will discuss the servant-leadership power of the Deborah anointing.

Read chapter 5 of *The Deborah Anointing,* "Deborah the Honeybee."

On the journey to embracing the Deborah anointing we must evaluate our interactions with others. We must evaluate our attitude and the words we use when working with those we are privileged to lead. Assessing our words and hearts toward others helps us as modern-day Deborahs become strong leaders who can usher others into their God-ordained calling.

Use the following assessment to evaluate your interactions with others. Read each statement, and select the answer that matches your thoughts concerning the scenario. Answer honestly with your first thought. Do not respond based on the way you would like to be or how you think the statement should be answered. Be as honest as possible as you measure your interaction with others.

You overhear a member of your church telling a pastoral counselor about problems she is having in her marriage. She is very upset. Would you tell your friends?

A. No, I do not know her, and it would be creepy to spread her bad news.

B. Well, maybe I would tell my closest friends and swear them to secrecy.

C. Sure. Maybe my friends can pray for this couple.

D. Why would I even remotely be interested in invading her privacy?

The filing cabinet is next to the manager's office. You're putting some documents away when you overhear your cruel manager bragging that he is springing a recertification test on your department tomorrow. You:

A. Make sure to put your notes in your handbag— you will need to study hard tonight.

B. Pass the word along to only your friends in the department so they will have an edge.

C. Freak out and then run through the office warning every employee you see.

D. Resolve to do your best on the quiz. You are not going to cram, and you are not going to tell anyone either.

The church grapevine, known for spreading gossip, is:

A. Best taken with a grain of salt.

B. An important way to keep one step ahead of possible changes.

C. Growing out of your section of the church.

D. A frivolous and irritating distraction from the real work of the church.

Your single friend Ann has a new boyfriend, named Matthew. One afternoon you are out picking up groceries. You see Matthew near the dairy section holding hands with a woman who is definitely not Ann. Do you tell anyone?

A. Not a chance. I do not want to be involved in anyone's breakup.

B. I might tell Ann privately. I am not sure how she will react, but her feelings count the most.

C. Of course! I will tell Ann in front of all my friends so everyone knows Matthew's a loser!

D. No way! I wouldn't touch such a tawdry situation with a ten-foot pole.

Gossip is:

A. Wrong, but tempting.

B. A harmless way of passing the time.

C. My very lifeblood.

D. Completely beneath me.

Psst. **Can you be trusted with a secret?**

A. I am not into secrets. I would rather not even hear them in the first place.

B. Sometimes. If it is a really close friend's secret, I can keep it totally to myself.

C. No, I have tried, but I just cannot keep secrets. Secrets eventually find their way slipping out of my mouth and into someone else's ears.

D. You bet. I pride myself in keeping secrets securely under my cap.

Your neighbors are having a loud argument upstairs. What do you do?

A. Ignore their argument.

B. Try to figure out what the argument is about.

C. Take notes—your neighbor downstairs is probably missing a lot of this.

D. Find something else to do but keep an ear peeled for anything that sounds violent.

Use the following rubric to measure your assessment.

Give one point for every A answer.

Give two points for every B answer.

Give three points for every C answer.

Give four points for every D answer.

Add the points you have received for each answer together to assess your interactions with others.

+ **Closed Shop** (up to 7)

  Gossip just is not your style. This is great! Take the time to engage in conversations with others through which you can share life-giving and encouraging words. Focus your conversations on positive talk that serves others and is encouraging to the soul.

+ **In the Mill** (8–14)

  You are probably the first to admit that when it comes to sharing others' information, you're only human. Sure, your ears perk up when you catch wind of some juicy information. You may even be known for publicly vocalizing your thoughts about other people. This may seem harmless since it is not your intention to hurt anyone and causing someone else pain is the last thing you want to do. However, there are always consequences to sharing others' private information, and no matter what your intentions are, gossiping is wrong. Always strive to respect the feelings of others.

+ **Big-Time Busybody** (15–21)

An obsession with gossip is trouble. Consider for a moment why you love being a part of everyone's story. Spend time in worship, asking God to minister to this broken place of your heart. You have the power to influence others in a positive way, and sharing others' news with everyone you meet is not a good way to use your influence or serve others.

+ **Lead Others on the Way** (22 and up)

You consider yourself to be on higher ground—miles above petty rumors. Your desire to avoid hurtful speech is admirable. Be sure to consistently moderate your attitude to assure that you are not presenting an attitude of superiority to others, but an attitude that welcomes others to become Christlike in their speech and attitude.

 *If you have not done so already, take time to watch lesson 3, "Becoming a Servant." Use the space below to take notes.*

_____

_____

_____

_____

Honeybee vs. Wasp

Becoming a woman of influence who leads others includes the call to be a servant. A servant leader is the call of a Deborah. Modern-day women embracing the call and anointing of Deborah ought to desire to model servant leadership. A servant leader is always mindful of how she interacts with others.

Every woman seeking to embrace the Deborah anointing should desire to interact with people like a honeybee and not like a wasp. A wasp looks a lot like a honeybee, but it is more aggressive in nature. Wasps don't produce anything. They fly around in search of food and will sting you if you get in the way. Honeybees, on the other hand, feed on nectar from plants so they can produce honey. They sting only when they have to, as a defense mechanism; their real mission is to produce honey, a sweet substance that is used to sustain others.[1] Those who are to walk in Deborah's anointing must examine their interactions with others to determine whether they are acting like wasps or honeybees.

Review the results from the last assessment. According to the assessment, how do you interact with people?

_____

_____

Do you think the assessment accurately captured your interaction with others? Why or why not?

_____

_____

According to your reading of chapter 5 in *The Deborah Anointing*, "Deborah the Honeybee," what are the characteristics of a wasp? How would you define these traits? Share an example of a time when you may have experienced these qualities in your life or in your interaction with others.

_____

_____

_____

_____

What are the character traits of a honeybee?

_____

_____

_____

_____

List the qualities of both the wasp and honeybee that you can honestly say you possess.

_____

_____

_____

_____

WORKER BEE PLAN

Having the qualities of a wasp keeps us from serving God's people and being able to transform and change lives to the glory of God. The inability to serve people keeps us from fulfilling our call as modern-day Deborahs. Build a plan to overcome wasp qualities using the Word of God, prayer, and worship. Once you have identified your wasp qualities, write down the honeybee qualities that you must cultivate to overcome this wasp nature. For example, if the wasp quality you recognize in your life is idleness, then consider cultivating motivation. Research scriptures concerning the honeybee qualities you desire for God to cultivate within you. Spend time in prayer and worship as you study the Word of God. Journal how you have noticed your nature changing as you submit your character to God in worship, the Word, and prayer.

BEE INFORMED *If you have not done so already, go back to the video to watch the conclusion of lesson 3, "Becoming a Servant." Use the space below to take notes.*

_____

_____

_____

_____

_____

_____

SERVANT LEADERS' SERVICE AREA

The day of the prima donna prophetess is over! God is calling women to become servant leaders in every sector of society. Whether you are in business, government, education, health care, ministry, or arts and entertainment, or if you're a stay-at-home mom, God is calling you to embrace servanthood. Servant leaders will seek to serve God's people; they will not look for God's people to serve them and their agendas. Those who seek to embrace the Deborah anointing are called to service and to operate as servant leaders in every area of their lives.

Deborah served God's people as a judge, deliverer, mother, warrior, and prophetess. In the same manner, modern-day Deborahs must serve God's people by:

- Listening
- Leading

- Being interested in others' well-being
- Moving in power

In each of these areas of service those operating in the Deborah anointing can bring glory to God and demonstrate His love and power to others.

SWEET WISDOM

Servant leaders will seek to serve God's people; they will not look for God's people to serve them and their agendas.

SERVE BY LISTENING

How well do you listen? Are you an active listener? When others speak, are you listening for comprehension, or solely to determine how to respond to the speaker?

_____

_____

_____

Here is an exercise to strengthen your active-listening skills. Place a blindfold on your eyes. Grab a friend, and have her share with you in detail a story you have never heard before. When your friend is done, remove the blindfold and recount every detail of the story.

How well did you listen to the details? Did you add details that were not previously mentioned? What details did you forget to include? Now check for comprehension. What was the takeaway of the story?

_____

_____

_____

Wait ten minutes, and recount the details of the story to your friend again. How many details did you remember this time? Repeat this activity with other friends to continue practicing active listening.

_____

_____

_____

As a servant leader, your ability to listen to others is key. Deborah sat for hours under the palm tree listening to the concerns of her community. She was an active listener with the ability to fully concentrate, understand, respond, and remember what others communicated to her. Using the wisdom of God, she could judge accurately the message behind what she was hearing. Review chapter 2 in *The Deborah Anointing*, "Deborah: The Judge and Deliverer," to gain more insight into the servant-leadership quality of listening.

SERVE BY LEADING

What opportunities have you had to lead others by serving as an organizer, facilitator, or director?

_____

_____

_____

Deborah was interested in others' growth, and she accomplished this by leading God's people. Leading requires organizing, facilitating, and directing God's people. Deborah served Barak by commissioning him to organize an army, helping to facilitate his ability to hear God's plan, and directing him to lead the people of Israel to victory over their enemy. Embracing the Deborah anointing calls for a deep interest in the growth of others and a commitment to zealously lead people to fulfill their calling. Review chapter 2 in *The Deborah Anointing*, "Deborah: The Judge and Deliverer," to gain more insight into the call to serve by leading.

SERVE BY BEING INTERESTED IN OTHERS' WELL-BEING

How do you nurture others? Whom are you specifically investing in during this season of your life?

_____

_____

_____

One of the major responsibilities of a modern-day Deborah is to bring the heart and mind of God in the earth by nurturing others. As a servant leader, Deborah was interested in the well-being of others. She was committed to consistently loving people, providing sound judgment, and living out her call as a prophetess and judge. Modern-day Deborahs must embrace the call to be like mothers and become a wellspring of life to others. Review chapter 3 in *The Deborah Anointing*, "Deborah the Mother," to gain more insight into the servant-leadership quality of investing in the growth of others.

SERVE BY MOVING IN POWER

What are some things you can do to be more intentional about sharing the voice of the Lord and the power of the Word of God with your family, your community, and those in your sphere of influence?

_____

_____

_____

Spend time listening, watching, waiting, and finding God's voice for your family, your community, and those in your sphere of influence. Use Scripture and forth-telling (communicating the mind of God for the present) or foretelling prophecy (communicating the mind of God for the future) to share the voice of the Lord with those individuals. Journal about what God led you to share.

_____

_____

_____

Embracing the Deborah anointing is a call to proclaim God's will to God's people. Deborah arose and served the people in power. She had the spirit of counsel and might on her side to overcome every weapon of her enemy.

The Deborah anointing is a call for women to preach, pray, and prophesy the Word of the Lord to their families, in their communities, and within their spheres of influence. Arise and serve God's people through forth-telling and foretelling prophecy. Use the authority God has given you to serve those around you. Review chapter 6 in *The Deborah Anointing*, "Deborah the Prophetess," to gain more insight into the call to serve by moving in power.

WORKER BEE PLAN

Review the four ways modern-day Deborahs are called to serve God's people. In which of these areas do you need the most improvement? Use the following questions to help you devise a plan to become a better servant leader.

Why do you believe this is your weakest area of service? Find some scriptures to encourage you as you seek God to help you strengthen your servant leadership.

_____

_____

_____

_____

_____

What is one thing you can do in this particular area to help you become a better servant leader? Identify training or other resources you can use to strengthen your servant-leadership capabilities.

_____

_____

_____

TRAITS OF A SERVANT LEADER

Deborah was a true servant leader. Because she was willing to follow God, she served others by leading them to liberty and freedom. She served her family, Barak, those who came under her palm tree for justice, and the nation of Israel. Deborah provides modern-day women with a model of the personality and character traits of a leader who is committed to serve. Women embracing the Deborah anointing to serve should be known by their ability to:

+ Restore value to people

+ Organize

+ Demonstrate compassion and mercy

+ Embrace femininity in leadership

+ Possess integrity and courage

Use the following questions to assess how your personality and character traits align with the qualities of a Deborah who is called to be a servant leader.

RESTORE VALUE TO PEOPLE

Why do you think the ability to restore others is a necessary trait for servant leaders?

_____

_____

_____

How do you foresee yourself restoring value to others?

_____

_____

_____

How are you currently restoring value to others?

_____

_____

_____

What are ways you can seek to restore value to others on a daily basis?

_____

_____

_____

Deborah arose at a time when the people of Israel were in bondage and being harassed by their enemies. She restored value to the people by reminding them of the power of their

God. Modern-day women are called to restore value to people by bringing them the hope of Jesus Christ. Serve others by sharing with them God's love and leading them to the hope of salvation found only in Jesus Christ.

ORGANIZE

What does the ability to organize look like within your sphere of influence?

_____

_____

_____

_____

If bringing structure and order is not your strong suit, what can you do to improve your organizational skills?

_____

_____

_____

_____

The ability to bring structure and order can look different depending on whether you are in the marketplace, the ministry, or the home. However, the principles are the same for women embracing the Deborah anointing—it is a call to organize by motivating, leading, directing, and facilitating.

Demonstrate compassion and mercy

Journal about a time when you demonstrated compassion and mercy to others.

_____

_____

_____

The Deborah anointing is also a calling to mother. How have you seen this trait operating in your life?

_____

_____

_____

What is one way you can remind yourself to operate in the love of a mother while sharing compassion and mercy with those you meet?

_____

_____

_____

The anointing to mother is not only for those who have children. Mothering is the ability to nurture others into the life God designed for them. Mothers come in all shapes, sizes, and circumstances.

EMBRACE FEMININITY IN LEADERSHIP

Describe your favorite female leader. Does this individual embody femininity to you?

_____

_____

_____

_____

Do you feel pressure to be more masculine in your leadership style? Why or why not?

_____

_____

_____

_____

What is something you can do to become more feminine in your leadership style?

_____

_____

_____

_____

Femininity is power and authority under control. Embrace the uniqueness of your femininity as you lead others.

Femininity is power and authority under control.

SWEET WISDOM

POSSESS INTEGRITY AND COURAGE

How would you define *integrity* and *courage*?

_____

_____

_____

_____

Why do you think integrity and courage are important traits for leaders to possess?

_____

_____

_____

_____

Integrity and courage are markers of our relationship with God and others. A woman of integrity is trustworthy before God and will possess the courage to arise and see God's vision come to pass for those she serves.

WORKER BEE PLAN

God created you to be a servant leader! Modern-day women who are called to embrace the Deborah anointing must possess the same traits that characterized the servant leadership of Deborah. Spend a moment looking in the servant's mirror using the following exercise.

Write down four verbs you would use to describe yourself. Ask a friend, spouse, or relative to do the same.

_____

_____

_____

What qualities did others use to describe you? Are their words similar to the verbs you used to describe yourself?

_____

_____

_____

Which of these verbs are traits of the honeybee?

_____

_____

_____

_____

Were you surprised by any of the verbs others used to describe you? Why or why not?

_____

_____

_____

_____

_____

Identify some ways you can strengthen your heart to serve. Employ these ideas in your next opportunity to serve.

_____

_____

_____

_____

_____

What is the greatest lesson you've learned from this session? How will you implement this takeaway to improve your servant leadership?

_____

_____

_____

_____

_____

Lesson 4

REPRODUCE

Where there is no vision [no redemptive revelation of God], the people perish.

—PROVERBS 29:18, AMPC

In this lesson you will evaluate the lifelong commitment of your calling.

Read chapters 10 and 11 of *The Deborah Anointing*.

The Deborah anointing is a call that will leave a legacy because it requires a commitment to reproduce. Those who will walk in Deborah's anointing are embracing a call to leave their mark upon the earth. By fulfilling their destiny today, modern-day Deborahs will be sowing a seed for the next generation to harvest for their betterment.

Thousands of years later the life and ministry of Deborah are still inspiring women and leading them into their purpose. You are called to have the same impact as Deborah's life has. You are called to impact people for generations to come, and leaving that legacy starts with having a vision to reproduce.

BUILDING A PATTERN TO REPRODUCE

What do you believe is needed to build a legacy?

_____

_____

_____

The ability to reproduce begins with a vision—a vision of hope, light, deliverance, and freedom that is not just for you but also for others.

In your own words, define the term *vision*.

_____

_____

_____

What is the origin of a vision? How are visions communicated to the vision-bearer?

_____

_____

_____

Read Habakkuk 2:2–3. How does this passage further inform your understanding of a God-given vision?

_____

_____

_____

Once we have received a vision, what is the most effective way to articulate that vision? Refer to Habakkuk 2:2–3 for clues.

_____

_____

_____

WORKER BEE PLAN

Vision comes from God. It addresses a burden of God or a present need, or it prepares us to move in God's compassion. Spend time praying and asking God to provide further details of your God-ordained assignment.

Take time to write out the vision God has given you to fulfill. Write down as much of your vision as you can.

_____

_____

_____

BEE INFORMED

If you have not done so already, take time to watch lesson 4, "Reproduce." Use the space below to take notes.

_____

_____

_____

_____

_____

God's Vision Lives in Me!

Writing your vision—and, most importantly, making it plain—allows others to come alongside you and participate in the legacy God desires to bring forth through you. SMART goals are specific, measurable, attainable, relevant, and time-specific. This can serve as an excellent blueprint for writing and communicating your vision. Use the questions below as a guide to help you articulate your God-given vision.

Specific

Begin by reviewing your vision from the previous exercise. Rewrite your vision, being as detailed and explicit as possible.

_____

_____

_____

_____

Measurable

How will you measure whether you have accomplished your goal?

_____

_____

_____

_____

What challenges do you foresee in accomplishing this vision?

_____

_____

_____

_____

ATTAINABLE

Is this vision achievable? What is something you can do to ensure you reach your God-given goal?

_____

_____

_____

_____

RELEVANT

How does this vision align with the passions of your heart?

_____

_____

_____

_____

TIME-SPECIFIC

What is the time frame God has given you to accomplish this vision?

_____

_____

_____

_____

_____

_____

_____

What makes the timeline to achieve your vision realistic? Is there another time frame that is more realistic? Why or why not?

_____

_____

_____

_____

_____

_____

_____

_____

Worker Bee Plan

A vision that is specific, measurable, attainable, realistic, and time-bound is a dream in action. What details are still missing from your vision blueprint? Spend time in prayer and worship asking God for additional details. Use the space provided to add these additional details to your SMART vision.

_____

_____

_____

_____

_____

_____

_____

Circle of Influence

God's vision living within your heart has the power to transform the world and those within your sphere of influence. Deborah's sphere of influence just happened to be her nation. Modern-day Deborahs have different levels of influence, but the commitment to releasing God's kingdom on the earth must remain the same. In implementing your vision, it is important to identify, understand, and clearly articulate the sphere of influence God has called you to transform.

List the individual(s) God has given you the power to influence. Refer to page 112 in *The Deborah Anointing* for the definition of *influence.*

_____

_____

_____

The group you just listed is considered your sphere of influence. A sphere of influence comprises the people, field, or area over which you have the power, through the Holy Spirit, to affect events, beliefs, behaviors, characteristics, and various types of development.

How are you stewarding your influence?

_____

_____

_____

_____

Deborah stewarded her influence through worship and prayer as well as by maintaining her integrity as a servant leader. God gives us the ability to influence others not to further our agenda but to point them toward the kingdom of God. Modern-day Deborahs will find their confidence to steward their influence by pursuing God's presence and moving in the power of the Holy Spirit. The more we pursue God, the more God will expand our sphere of influence.

Modern-day Deborahs will find their confidence to steward their influence by pursuing God's presence and moving in the power of the Holy Spirit.

Have you noticed God expanding your influence? Refer to the list on pages 114–116 of *The Deborah Anointing* to identify the prophetic instructions for enlarging your boundaries of influence. Which of these instructions have you noticed God using to expand your influence?

_____

_____

_____

God's desire is to increase us extravagantly. God will expand our influence through wisdom, preaching, teaching, increased authority, and collaboration.

Read Isaiah 54:1–3. Which of these prophetic instructions do you believe God is calling you to follow in this season?

_____

_____

_____

BEE INFORMED *If you have not done so already, go back to the video to watch the conclusion of Lesson 4, "Reproduce." Use the space below to take notes.*

_____

_____

_____

_____

_____

_____

Go Forth and Reproduce

The mandate for modern-day women embracing the Deborah anointing is to reproduce. Deborah had a vision from the Lord that she could clearly articulate. As she articulated God's vision within her sphere of influence, Deborah was able to see that vision move into action and begin to reproduce in the hearts of others. Likewise, modern-day women are called to reproduce God's vision in others' hearts.

Reproducing God's vision will often require collaboration with those both in your current generation and in future generations. Deborah had a large vision from the Lord to deliver the people of Israel from their cruel enemies. She could not accomplish this vision on her own. God called her to enlist Barak, Israel's army, and even a housewife named Jael to be involved in realizing His vision of freedom for the nation. Consider for a moment the individuals God is calling you to partner with to accomplish your God-given vision.

Who are the partners you need to achieve your God-given vision?

_____

_____

_____

Which of these individuals are already present in your sphere of influence?

_____

_____

_____

Are there individuals in your sphere of influence who can connect you with the other people you need to fulfill God's vision?

_____

_____

_____

Review chapter 7 in *The Deborah Anointing*, "Deborah and Barak," especially pages 71–75. Create a list of the effective elements of collaboration. How will you apply these elements in your current partnerships?

_____

_____

_____

Reproducing God's vision can start with collaboration or mentorship. The Deborah anointing calls women to build a legacy by mentoring the next generation. Mentoring gives modern-day women the ability to nurture others by imparting within them godly character and wisdom. Every woman should have someone else she is actively pouring into, empowering with wisdom, and training to carry God's vision. Scripture is filled with examples of mentoring relationships.

One example is that of Elijah and Elisha found in the Books of 1 and 2 Kings. Elijah and Elisha were prophets in different generations. God gave Elijah a vision, which was always to have someone represent the voice of the Lord to the nation of Israel. To fulfill God's vision, Elijah began speaking as the voice of the Lord for the nation as well as mentoring Elisha. Eventually, when Elijah's time was completed on earth, God's vision continued in Israel through Elisha. This was a direct result of Elijah's taking the time to mentor Elisha. Thus, God's vision to have a representation of His voice among the nation continued beyond Elijah's life.

Read Titus 2:3–5. According to this Scripture passage, why is mentorship important?

_____

_____

_____

_____

Are you currently mentoring? If you currently do not have a mentee, begin to pray and ask God to lead you to someone whom you can help mature in the Word and the call of God.

Use the space provided to journal about what God speaks to you.

_____

_____

_____

_____

WORKER BEE PLAN

Read Philippians 3:14. How will you continue to press toward achieving the vision God gave you even after this study is complete?

_____

_____

_____

_____

LIVE OUT YOUR CALL!

Embracing the Deborah anointing is much like achieving your God-given vision. Both are ongoing activities and not just a means to an end. Modern-day Deborahs must intentionally build confidence, dwell in the presence of God through worship, lead through serving, and reproduce on a regular basis by setting SMART goals.

Spend time reviewing your workbook. Ensure that all the Worker Bee Plans you created were implemented successfully.

This may be the end of this study, but it's the beginning of a new level of power and influence. May the blessings of the Lord be with you as you continue your journey to live out your call to be a modern-day Deborah.

NOTES

Lesson 1: Process the Call

1. *Oxford Living Dictionaries*, s.v. "embrace," accessed February 16, 2017, https://en.oxforddictionaries.com/definition/us/embrace.

2. *Merriam-Webster's Collegiate Dictionary*, eleventh edition (Springfield, MA: Merriam-Webster Inc., 2003), s.v. "time."

Lesson 2: The Power of Worship

1. Bible Study Tools, s.v. "*proskuneō*," accessed February 17, 2017, http://www.biblestudytools.com/lexicons/greek/kjv/proskuneo.html.

Lesson 3: Becoming a Servant

1. Jennifer Horton, "What's the Difference Between Bees and Wasps," How Stuff Works, accessed February 17, 2017, http://animals.howstuffworks.com/insects/bee-vs-wasp1.htm.

ABOUT THE AUTHOR

Michelle McClain-Walters has traveled to more than fifty nations and has conducted prophetic schools that have activated thousands in the art of hearing God's voice. The author of *The Deborah Anointing*, *The Esther Anointing*, and *The Prophetic Advantage*, Michelle currently serves as director of prayer ministry at Crusaders Church, under the leadership of Apostle John Eckhardt. She is an international and national conference speaker. She is also an apostolic team leader for The Impact Network. Michelle resides in Chicago with her husband, Pastor Floyd A. Walters Jr.

CONNECT WITH US!

CHARISMA HOUSE

(Spiritual Growth)

Facebook.com/CharismaHouse

@CharismaHouse

Instagram.com/CharismaHouse

SILOAM

(Health)

Pinterest.com/CharismaHouse

MODERN ENGLISH VERSION

(Bible)

www.mevbible.com